Pretty Brown Girl

Written By Christina Louise

Copyright ©2019 by Christina Worth

All rights reserved.

No part of this book may be reproduced or transmitted in any form or by any means, electronic or mechanical, including photocopying, recording, or by any information storage and retrieval system, without permission in writing from the copyright author, except for the use of brief quotations in a book review.

ISBN: 978-1-970135-36-7   paperback

Published in the United States by Pen2Pad Ink Publishing.

Christina Louise retains the right to all images.

Pretty brown girl...
You are created on purpose
with a purpose to change the world.

Pretty brown girl...
You are gentle yet strong,
shy yet bold,
broken yet beautiful.

Pretty brown girl...
You are one of a kind
with a beautiful mind.

Pretty brown girl...
You can be anything you desire to be
so let no one dim your light.

Pretty brown girl...
You are greater than the no's
you will hear throughout life.
They are merely steppingstones
to your destiny.

Pretty brown girl...
You are complex yet simple.
You will stand out
even when you try to blend in.

Pretty brown girl...
You are a survivor.
The bad things you have experienced
or may experience do not define you.

Pretty brown girl...
You are enough and worthy of love.

Pretty brown girl...
You are amazing, flaws and all.

Pretty brown girl...
You are the only version of you
the world will know
so be your best truest you!!!